I0162236

Chronicles of an Armor Bearer
ISBN-10: 978-1-7358756-3-7
LOC #: 2020919219
Fiery Beacon Publishing House, LLC
Greensboro, North Carolina, USA

© 2020 by Donnalee M. Peet

Published 2020

Chronicles
of an
ARMOR BEARER

"You are first a child of God,

and then a servant".

DONNALEE PEET

Fiery Beacon
PUBLISHING HOUSE

Table of Contents

Acknowledgements
The Dedication
The Blessing
Introduction

Acknowledgements

Thank you to Bishop Neil C. Ellis and the Mount Tabor Church family for allowing me the privilege to work and serve as I grew in God.

To my husband, Wesley L. Peet Sr. Thank you for your support and for encouraging me, pushing me in this endeavor. To my sons Danny Jr. and Dinero for the many nights you both waited up for me to complete my assignment, thank you; may God continue to keep you and us covered.

To Lady Shandlene Parker Grant for the honor to serve you for more than twenty-five years as a friend, sister, and armor-bearer. Lady, you "rock!" Thank you!

The Dedication

This book is dedicated to my spiritual mother Evangelist Lady Carnetta Ferguson. She taught me the discipline of armor-bearing from the initial stages and allowed me the opportunity to serve her with a spirit of excellence. Her example demanded nothing but the best.

She is an educator, evangelist, business professional, counselor, mother, and, until his recent passing, the faithful wife to her earthly god—as she would say—the distinguished minister, administrator, educator, and former senator W. J. Ferguson. One would learn how to walk in any of these roles just by watching the way "Mother Carn" would defuse a situation. This unique woman of God is a sniper in the army of God, winning thousands to Christ with her commitment to the call on her life. One will always find safety being in her presence. Her home is always a place of welcome, full of laughter and joy.

Thank you for affording me the privilege to walk with you, Mother Carn. I recall you saying to me, "Donna, I see you in deep waters; I pray you can swim." May this book depict what I have learned from you.

To my earthly mother, Dorcas Elizabeth Cox, a woman of extraordinary talents, a mentor in her own rank who showed me how to believe in myself. She also showed me that learning is the greatest tool in life, no matter the age, when, at the age of fifty-five, she walked through the hall of a college to obtain undergraduate and graduate degrees in mortuary science. Mom, may the favor of God continually be your portion, a woman of grace and favor!

The Blessing

Donnalee is a woman of much wisdom, love, time and perfection. The very thought of something out of order or needing to be fixed causes her juices to bubble and before you know it, the assignment is complete, and she is long gone and unseen. This can be considered one of the valuable characters of an Armorbearer. The art of Servitude is embodied in the attitude, spirit and function of this gifted author. Consistency breeds reliability in her workflow and the product of her service. Truly after thirty-seven years of Hospitality and Servant Leadership, the outcome of laying down one's life and taking care of people is not superficial but an innate ability, a gift passed down from generation of Servants to her. The Bearing of Arms for more than thirty years and working between multiple personalities have definitely qualified her to share her thoughts and give simple guidance to other people who bear arms.

Pastor Shandlene R. Grant

Universal Household of Faith Community Holiness Church

Women of Virtue and Integrity Empowerment Group,
Founder and President

Introduction

I grew up in a Pentecostal church, where holiness was the order of the day. You attended five services on a Sunday — sunrise prayer meeting, morning Sunday school, and divine service all before 11:00 a.m., then afternoon Sunday school and evening service 7:00 p.m. Young ladies were not allowed to wear trousers nor jewelry and makeup. As a result of all of this, by the time I was sixteen, I was all churched out.

Years later, I found myself running back to the very thing I had run from — the church. I accepted the call and devoted and applied myself to every area of ministry, including the choir, children's church, the hospital department, and evangelism. But it was in the evangelism department that I met my first mentor, Evangelist Carnetta Ferguson, known to many by the name "Mother Carn." This woman of God had a zeal about her that would draw you in. As I became jointly fitted to her preaching and teacher style, she began to teach me about the Word of God. She ministered and traveled with a team, which I became a member of, and it was at this time that the need arose for an *adjutant* or *armor-bearer*.

Back then, I had never heard of an armor-bearer, nor did I know what the position entailed. The assignment of working alongside this vessel of honor was given to me, and there began my training. Her ministry took her to many conferences, ministries, and other assignments in the church world. During our travels to different ministries, I learned that not every leader had an adjutant; therefore, it was difficult for me to know if I was performing my role correctly. I needed knowledge; I want to stay current, as the decade of the nineties was coming to an end.

As an armor-bearer, things are constantly changing around you; so, it is vital that you be ever learning, building and enhancing yourself. The goal is to cover your leader as you help to fortify the Kingdom of God through your service. At the end of 1996, I transitioned to another ministry, Mount Tabor Full Gospel Baptist Church, as it was known back then, and there I met Pastor Delton Ellis and received training in the field of servanthood. My purpose and destiny guided me to another gift to the body of Christ, one Shandlene

R. Parker-Grant, with whom I was able to enhance my knowledge and carry out my assignment. What I have learned through the years from these anointed vessels is what I have penned in this training guide.

Chapter 1

Chosen for Service

What is an Armor-Bearer?

An *armor-bearer* is one who bears arms; one who protects. The armor-bearer serves his/her pastor or leader in any way possible. He/she is also referred to as an adjutant, who acts as a personal assistant to the leader. In biblical times, armor-bearers carried the shield or other weapons of the king. Their main duty was to protect the warrior in the time of battle. To put it into modern terms, the main duty of the armor-bearer is to protect the leader during spiritual conflict.

For biblical accounts of armor-bears, please read the following scriptures

1 Samuel 14:1   1 Samuel 16:21   1 Samuel 31:4-5

1 Chronicles 10:4-5   1 Chronicles 11:39

****

From the beginning of time the Father created each of us in His image and likeness. We were created to solve a problem or to be an answer to someone's problem; we were not designed to be the problem. You are the answer to someone's problem. Find your purpose, and what you do will appear to be natural or will be easy for you to accomplish. One of my favorite encouragements is to find out why you were created. What is your purpose? Our journey through this life leads us to different paths: some of us enjoy public speaking, others teaching, still others writing poetry or even a novel. Others are born to be leaders, pastors, accountants, lawyers, and so on. Wherever our path leads us, the Holy Spirit is there as a guide to lead us into all truths.

We know ourselves better than anyone does; we know our likes and dislikes. "To thine own self be true" is a wise admonition. Your light will either draw persons to you or cause them to stay away from you. Your personality speaks loudly and tells people whether you are a person that would make a good leader.

Most persons see an armor-bearer and think the role means a life of glamour, being in the forefront, a person who is walking along with the man/woman of God, carrying their Bible or their materials. Some see this work as "Lights, Camera, Action!" never understanding what an armor-bearer is or does.

An armor-bearer is a calling. Each of us is placed here on the earth to carry out an assignment. Your man/woman of God has seen the gift of servitude on your life. A call to armor-bearing is a privilege and is full of excitement, knowing that you have been chosen to accompany the servant of God who is the mouthpiece of God, declaring the unadulterated word of God. This is the person you have been given the honor to serve.

Serving as an armor-bearer calls for a lot of sacrifice. You must be willing to meet the challenges that come with this position. Long nights away from your family, especially when your leader is ministering and your assignment is to be there until he/she completes their assignment. Sometimes you have to refrain from desserts and delicacies because you have been called to a time of prayer and fasting.

Sometimes, the role of the armor-bearer can be a lonely walk. You may have to isolate yourself because of the call and the demand that is placed on your life. Friends and associates may not be traveling on the same path. Spending time with God becomes a priority and the **calling that you are now walking in is God-centered.**

Reflection

Are you an individual with great leadership skills? Can you be trusted to carry out instructions? Can you handle criticism? Are you able to make a decision on your own?

A Servant's Heart

When the mother of Zebedee's sons went to the Master requesting that her sons sit on the right side and left in His Kingdom, she was not expecting His response. He (Jesus) pointed out what it takes to be placed in those positions.

"But Jesus called them to Himself and said, 'You know that the rulers of the Gentile lord it over them, and those who are great authority over them. Yet it shall not be so among you; but whoever desires to become great among you, let him be your servant. And whoever desire to be first among you, let him be your slave—Just as the Son of Man did not come to be served, but to serve, and to give His life a ransom for many.'"

Matthew 20:25-28

***

What Does It Mean to Serve?

To *serve* is to perform a duty or service for another person or an organization; to obey, assist, help, benefit, do something for.

Not everyone has the capacity to serve or to be a servant. One has to be broken and anointed by the Holy Spirit. A servant has humility, and one who is devoted to the call must be submitted and committed. When you are submitted to something, you accept it; you surrender to the process. Being committed is to put your trust in what you believe or to be dedicated to a thing.

It was exciting to serve alongside the Woman of God, but I had to be anointed to keep up with Mother Carn (smile). While ministering (preaching and teaching), she would stand on chairs, run around the room barefoot. She would pray for folks and they would receive their healing.

21

Her unique style and zeal as she ministered the Word of God was very energetic. Being under the anointing, one is equipped with supernatural strength; but as you descend your physical body becomes weak, and this is where the need for an armor-bearer comes in. As one who is called to protect, shield, pray and cover your leader when they are most vulnerable.

When wisdom enters your heart,
And knowledge is pleasant to your soul,
Discretion will preserve you;
Understanding will keep you...

Proverbs 2:10-11

Keys

❖ **Remain close enough** that you can see when your leader gives you a signal to draw close.

❖ **Pay attention to your leader's body language**. This would indicate that it is time to   move.

❖ **Watch for the sign.** This means that it is time to retrieve their items from the pulpit.

As a servant to your leader, you have the responsibility to ensure that everything is secured and nothing is left behind, laying around or exposed. You are accountable for everything that your leader has in his/ her possession. I accompanied my leader at a recent gathering, and while I did not sit near her, I was within range for us to see each other. While waiting on my leader at the end of the service, I had the opportunity to view other members of the clergy. There was a woman of God accompanied by a male adjutant, and as she mingled in the crowd, I realized that she had left her purse on the pulpit. It was her armor-bearer's responsibility to make sure that everything about her person was accounted for. I later learned that her purse had been misplaced. Some assignments call for a female armor-bearer, who would pay attention to small details such as a woman's purse or handbag.

❖ Check and Re-Check

- ❖ It would be a tragedy to arrive at an airport only to realize that something essential to your leader's ministry has been forgotten.

- ❖ A leader should have an adjutant/armor-bearer who understands his/her needs precisely, not leaving anything to chances.

- ❖ Ensure that all luggage is accounted for when traveling.

As a servant of God, your leader sees more than the ordinary person sees, but your leader is also human and needs to be guarded. You should not be so entangled with your surroundings that you miss when you're being called upon by your leader.

The boy Samuel ministered unto the Lord. In those days the Word of the LORD was rare and as he (Samuel) lay down he heard his name being called. After receiving the instruction from Eli, he answered the call saying to the LORD, "Speak, for Your servant hears,"

1 Samuel 3:10b

Samuel was listening to hear what was to be said to him; he also obeyed the instruction that was given to him. Samuel is a good example of how we should be willing to listen and ready to obey any instruction given and prepare to execute the instruction with excellence.

Being a servant is a greater call and having a servant's heart means even more!

Servanthood is a calling worthy of honor. Sometimes, the very person who is serving is overlooked. Do not allow being unnoticed to stop you from serving; instead, keep on serving and do it with excellence! Your service is unto God and not unto men.

And whatever you do, do it heartily, as to the Lord and not to men, knowing that from the Lord you will receive the reward of the inheritance; for you serve the Lord Christ.

Colossians 3:23-24

Keys

❖ Stay close to your leader because the oil that is on their life will fall upon you. Serve God fervently so that the anointing will stay fresh on your life.

❖ Be confident in how you serve your leader. Serve with humility and not with arrogance. **"Let your light so shine** before men, that they may see your good works and glorify your Father in heaven." -Matthew 5:16

❖ Serve with grace and wisdom. **"Grace and peace be yours in abundance through the knowledge of God and of Jesus our Lord." -1 Peter 1:2**

❖ Be strong and allow the Holy Spirit to direct your path. **"The steps of a good man are ordered by the Lord, And He delights in his way." -Psalm 37:23**

❖ Today's leaders need to have a heart for the very people they lead. Some are doing the right thing but for the wrong reasons. As representatives in the earth, we are to please God and not our flesh. **"So then, those who are in the flesh cannot please God" (Romans 8:8).**

❖ There is a difference between someone being a servant and being hired to serve.

❖ A servant will do his/her job from the heart and not expect anything in return. This does not mean that he/she should not be seeded into. Everyone enjoys feeling appreciated.

❖ The individual who is hired to do a job should expect to be paid for his/her work and labor. For the Scripture says: **"You shall not muzzle an ox while it treads out the grain"** (Deuteronomy 25:4) and **"The labor is worthy of his wages"** (1 Timothy 5:18).

❖ As a servant, you have been bought with a price. This means that you should be grounded in Christ; not every wind of doctrine should be able to entice you.

❖ It is best to have one leader speaking into your life than many voices in your hearing, which could cause confusion.

❖ Learn the art of serving and what it entails.

❖ Study the Word of God. Make it a habit to read a chapter or memorize a scripture verse daily. This is essential; the more of the Word you have within you, the better equipped you become.

> **Be diligent to present yourself approved to God, a worker who does not need to be ashamed, rightly dividing the word of truth.**
>
> **2 Timothy 2:15**

❖ Sharpen your discernment. This means that you have to map out your own prayer times. To discern, you must know the difference between good and evil; be able to recognize when something is out of place; and be able to perceive what is the next move. Pray and ask God for more revelation.

❖ Know the vision of the person that you are called to serve. Know what your personal visions and goals are and see how they align with the leader you are called to serve.

- ❖ As you serve, secrets are revealed to you. Others should never be able to see your leader in a vulnerable state. Yes, oh yes, leaders have bad moments, and yes, they also feel hurts and pains. Learn when to be quiet and when to speak; not everything requires a response.

- ❖ Your leader should not have to be concerned about you keeping things in their right perspective.

- ❖ Your leader should not have to be worried about whether his/her business will get out because of you. Trust is the order of the day: DO NOT BREACH IT.

A question you should ask yourself is this: "Do I believe in the vision of my leader? And am I prepared to carry out this assignment to the best of my ability?"

Czan two walk together unless they are agreed?
Amos 3:3

*Remember, you are first a child of God, then a servant.

■■

Reflection

1. **Do I possess a servant's heart?**

----

2. **What things ought I to pay close attention to?**

----

3. **What keys in this chapter do I need to work on? State how you intend to enhance them.**

----

4. **How has this chapter helped me?**

The Role of the Armor-Bearer

Your responsibility is great. You were chosen for the assignment because your leader saw greater in you. Now that you have been entrusted with this awesome task, stay humble and pure; obedience is the key to your succeeding.

Now it happened one day that Jonathan the son of Saul said to the young man who bore his armor, "Come, let us go over to the Philistines' garrison that is on the other side." But he did not tell his father.

1 Samuel 14:1

You must be willing to protect and fight with and for your leader. It may be hard at times, but you must be willing to support your leader's decisions. Your responsibilities call for you to be a quick thinker and always ready for action. We are in a spiritual war; you should always be on alert.

❖ An armor-bearer must be trustworthy. He/she ought to be able to adhere to the choices made by his/her leader and not release information.

❖ When your leader allows you to sit in a certain meeting, you must become invisible. You should be seen and not heard. Be cognizant of what is going on; your leader might want to discuss later what took place in the meeting. You may be able to give insight into something that might have been overlooked by your leader.

❖ Learn to read and discern body language, which is what is not being said or mentioned.

❖ Only when asked or when you are given the opportunity to respond to a question should you be seen. You are not there to give your input; use wisdom and be wise in your deportment.

❖ It is always best to be honest with your leader. If something is out of place, it is your duty to indicate what is wrong in a respectable manner.

❖ Remember, you are a reflection of your leader. Keep your deportment balanced and healthy.

❖ The leader's family is important to him/her and, therefore, should be important to you. Be cordial!

❖ Likewise, if you are married, your home is your priority. Make sure all areas of your home are covered before you leave to serve the man/woman of God. As a priority, your home is your sanctuary: ensure that everything is in alignment and covered.

❖ The unmarried armor-bearer has more time on his/her hands than one who is married. Enjoy your singleness as you serve. This is preparation for how you will serve your spouse when you get married.

❖ For an armor-bearer, to be punctual is to be ahead of time. You should have already communicated with the relevant persons to obtain the necessary information and requirements.

❖ An armor-bearer must be given to prayer and fasting. As you commune with the Father, He will guide you and give you strategies and ideas on how to serve and cover your leader. At times, especially when you are preparing for the next assignment, fasting will place you in a better position for areas that you will need to pay extra attention.

*Worship** will destroy any atmosphere.
* **Prayer and Fasting** open your ears to hear.
* **Prayer** deals with your hearing (ears).
* **Fasting** deals with your mouth (speaking).

- ❖ If your communication has been closed, fasting will cause there to be an open flow.

- ❖ An armor-bearer is to be one who is full of the Holy Spirit, and of good reputation, character, and moral values. He/She must also operate in a spirit of excellence.

Then this Daniel distinguished himself above the governors and satraps, because an excellent spirit was in him; and the King gave thought to setting him over the whole realm.

Daniel 6:3

This passage is loaded, but I want to focus on Daniel the person, who "distinguished himself." To *distinguish* is "to recognize a difference or to be identified as a characteristic of something or to earn a position of status or high esteem; it is also to discern." (Dictionary.com). This is the most important attribute of an armor-bearer, and the reason your leader chose you.

An armor-bearer should be a person of prayer and intercession. He/she should be prayed up, especially when on an assignment. Every territory has a different stronghold. You will need to know the area or region you have entered so that you can receive revelation, insight and instruction in your prayer time with the Father. This is where He will download His strategies to you.

Whoever loves instruction loves knowledge, But he who hates correction is stupid.

* * *

After service one evening, I recall a lady wanting to have a word with the woman of God. I had already received my instructions: she had already exceeded the maximum number of persons that she would interact with for the night. However, the lady insisted, saying that she was the woman of God's cousin. Nevertheless, I could not allow her access to Mother Carn; she became vexed and began spewing derogatory names; she even went as far as saying that she knew my parents and would be having a word with them. I stood my ground knowing that I had been given a directive. Even though I was told afterward that I could have allowed her access, Mother Carn was pleased to know that I had followed the instructions.

At times, it's hard to be that person who says, "not at this time" or "leave the message with me and I'll make sure that he/she gets it," but NO is a full sentence. Do not be afraid to use it.

****

Serving as an armor-bearer is not about carrying a bag for your leader; it is about having a pure motive and a pure heart to serve your leader. That's what makes for a good armor-bearer. Having a passion to make things easier should come naturally to you if your heart is in the right place.

❖ No one person has the monopoly on serving. You are ever learning, and as you travel from place to place with your leader, you WILL gain more knowledge. What was good in the nineties is not relevant today.

Reflection

1. **How can I serve my leader better?**

   ----

2. **What is the main characteristic of an armor-bearer? How can I enhance the knowledge that was gained through reading this charter?**

   ----

3. **How can I serve and develop a spirit of excellence?**

   ----

4. **How often do you fast and pray?**

Chapter 2:

How and Where to Serve

Knowing Your Leader

"Where are we going?"

This was my question to Mother Carn when she rang me. I had begun to settle into my new role as the woman of God's adjutant and was putting things in perspective. Whenever she traveled, one of my tasks was to visit the sight, area, or building of her assignment to check out the atmosphere. With the enabling of the Holy Spirit, I began to develop the ability to discern her likes and dislikes. For the leader/pastor, there is nothing like knowing there is someone in your corner, praying for you as you carry out the assignment that will bring glory to the Kingdom. Having someone who is there to push you, or a supporter who has some discernment of your assignment makes the assignment so much easier, as you can now focus on what you have been called to do.

As your leader's armor-bearer, you should be the first one to be in place where your leader is about to minister, primarily because you know what their expectations are and you are aware of their likes and dislikes, and, for example, the things that would distract them. Staying close to your leader and observing them closely will make it easier for you to learn his/her actions and body language. You must understand the ways of your leader.

Keys

❖ If there is a teammate working along with you, decide between yourselves who will serve where; this is not a competition. The mandate should be to bring honor and glory to God and, by extension, His Kingdom.

❖ Watch the way your leader deals with people and situations.

1. Who does the leader allow into his/her space?

2. Does the leader drink hot or cold beverages? Is this received before or after he/she has

   ministered?

3. Does the leader require a quiet atmosphere? Or will he/she engage in a conversation?

4. Would the leader want to interact with anyone before he/she ministers?

5. Will the leader's family be attending the service? Knowing this would enable you to make the seating arrangements. This will prevent the leader from having to scan the audience to locate his/her family. Assign someone to the family.

The Holy Spirit is a gentleman and is in control. Therefore, if you need to shout, do it and get back in position. You cannot be falling out under the power and your leader needs you. Stay focused and allow the Holy Spirit to do His work; but keep your eyes on your leader.

❖ Know where your leader's transportation is located in the event he/she wants to leave expeditiously. Make sure the vehicle's path is unobstructed.

❖ Make a mental list of these things as you begin serving your leader; for example, what and where are the leader's change of attire?

You are to ensure that you have a laundry bag for any wet clothing. (This should be on your checklist.)

❖ Will your leader be leaving directly after the services or will he/she stay and socialize? Will your leader require water, mints, lozenges? These items should be close to you to access. Have a travel bag that is large enough to contain these items as well as an extra Bible and towels.

❖ **Not every leader is the same in style**. In the case of a man of God, inquire of his spouse how she would like her husband to look and be assisted. You should NOT serve any leader and dislike the spouse. (Sit down!) They are one.

These are just a few of the questions you need to ask and things you should know in order to serve your leader more effectively. One of your main priorities should be to make your leader look good; this also includes your demeanor. There will be people watching to see how you and your leader communicate. Always show that there is togetherness; you have been chosen to walk alongside the man/woman of God, which is an honor and a privilege.

❖ **An armor-bearer is the second eye of the leader**. Make sure that you are prayed up.   There is no reason for you (who should be serving) to be on the prayer line with everyone else. It is of the utmost importance that you be in place assisting your leader.

❖ **Make time to have a one on one with your Leader so that he/she can pour into you.** This can happen while you are on the road to or from an assignment. Find the time so you can inquire about things that are not clear to you. Upgrading yourself is an essential part of your assignment and calling as an armor-bearer.

❖ **There should be a difference between serving with your leader and your leader's personal life**. The leader's personal life should remain private. Whatever he/she decides to do outside of ministry may not involve you. So, do not take it personally. Keeping your relationship in perspective will save you from a lot of disappointment, especially if there is a function that your leader may have been invited to and you weren't. You are there to serve not to be his/her friend. Give them breathing room. DO NOT cross that line. In fact, you should encourage your leader to enjoy his/her family because they are away from them a lot. Set boundaries for yourself.

****

Your Appearance and Dress Code

Don't you realize that your body is a temple of the Holy Spirit, who lives in you and was given to you by God? You do not belong to yourself, for God bought you with a high price. So, you must honor God with your body.
    —1 Corinthians 6: 19-20 NLT

As I stood on the outside of the door waiting for my leader to leave, I was approached by a young man wanting to drop off an envelope. When I inquired why he was giving it to me, he responded, "Aren't you the armor-bearer?" How did he know this? Was there something about the way I was dressed? Was I wearing a name tag explaining my position?

As a servant working alongside your leader, it is imperative that your appearance is not a distraction.

For Ladies:

1. Your clothing should not be too loose or too tight.

2. Dresses should not be too short. Your skirt's length is good when the skirt can cover your knees when you are seated.

3. Shirt/Blouse buttons should not be busting open at the chest/cleavage area, as this signifies that the top is too small or too tight. This can be a distraction.

4. If your skirt has a split, it is recommended that it be no more than 3 inches high.

5. A jacket gives you a more uniformed look.

6. You should always keep a shawl handy.

7. If you decide to wear a uniform, the recommended colors are black, navy, or grey.

8. Pantyhose give you a more professional look.

9. Always wear comfortable shoes.

10. Be modest in appearance: no loud makeup, jewelry, or clothing. Sometimes a female armor-bearer might need to be attired in a pantsuit. Be sure this choice lines up with the protocol of the place you are about to serve.

For Males:

1. A black, navy, or grey suit

2. Comfortable shoes

3. No loud-color shirt, socks, or ties

4. Modest haircut and nicely shaven

5. If you are a heavy-set man, be sure that your clothing is the right size and fits properly on your body.

Your dress code should be used to identify who you are, without anyone having to ask. Be sure to invest in your appearance and your wardrobe. Sometimes people will see you before they see your leader. So, dress for the assignment and not to be a distraction!

YOUR CHECKLIST

Here are the essential items you should have in your kit/ table as you serve your pastor/leader at events.

❑ Water
❑ Juice
❑ Notepad and pen
❑ Mints
❑ Hand/Paper Towel
❑ Towels
❑ Facial tissue, e.g. Kleenex
❑ Lozenges
❑ Drinking glass with cover
❑ Tithing /Love Offering envelope
❑ Extra glass (one for every person to be served).

TRAVEL KIT

❑ Towels with a wrap (to avoid touching towels before use)

❑ Bible

❑ Hand sanitizer

❑ Lozenges

❑ Water (Your leader may use a special brand of water.)

❑ Shoe cloth

❑ Shoe brush

❑ Proper luggage (Pack lightly for yourself so that you can assist your leader with his/her luggage.)

❑ Proper shoes

❑ Drinking glass with cover for exclusive use by your leader

❑ Your leader's teacup and choice of tea/coffee and sweetener (sugar or honey)

❑ Notepad and pen

❑ Extra money

❑ Pain reliever, e.g., Aspirin

❑ Sewing kit

❑ Reusable storage bags, e.g., Ziplock

❑ Box of facial tissue, e.g., Kleenex

❑ First aid kit

❑ Shawls or scarves

❑ Covering for a microphone

❑ Small travel size can of odor eliminator, e.g., Febreze

❑ Small travel size can of disinfectant, e.g., Lysol spray

It is always best to know the name of the city, the location of the church, and the living accommodations when you are traveling in the event your leader falls asleep and you are the designated driver.

Reflection

Who pays for your travel and accommodation?

The cost of travel and accommodation should be covered by your leader. Know that even though you are a servant, you are leaving your family, work/business to serve. This can take a toll on you physically, emotionally, and financially. If you are married, having a supportive spouse makes it easier for you to function in your role. As long as your spouse has released you to travel or accompany your leader, you are free to go forth. Before agreeing to the assignment, you should inquire of your leader about

expenses.

Chapter 3:

Serving Under Pressure

Do's and Don'ts of an Armor-Bearer

The armor-bearer is to be trustworthy and of good character. Be attentive and slow to speak. Not everything deserves a response.

So then, my beloved brethren, let every man be swift to hear, slow to speak, slow to wrath; for the wrath of man does not produce the

righteousness of God.

James 1:19

As a servant/ armor bearer when you realize that your season is over with your leader due to things such as:

- ❖ You are at an impasse,

- ❖ Your hearing has been blocked (you have allowed other to contaminate you with negatively)

- ❖ You have stopped seeking the face of God to know when to shift and change from the old thing into a fresh and new thing in God.

- ❖ You may be experiencing family issues and need to take a break for a while to fix the situation.

Know that as an armor bearer you need your time and sometimes continuously going and serving one can feel burnt-out. This is the time that you need to take a minute and step back so that you can be refreshed.

* Never leave a Ministry feeling hurt or having

unresolved issues. This is unhealthy for everyone. Even

if you left serving your leader, you are still a servant. Use

every negative situation as a learning process and leave

the door opens to communicate with your Leader at any

time. Speaking evil of a place which you served is a

negative reflection on you!

Keys

❖ Always have the correct information you may need to

correct a statement. Do not get into an argument or try

to defend your leader. How would your leader respond?

Put yourself in your leader's shoes and envision how

he/she would respond to the situation.

❖ Take on the posture of your leader; there is no need to be rude. Oftentimes, people are not nice; so, this is where your character comes in.

❖ Any message to be delivered to your leader should be forwarded through you. This is where your discernment is needed, that is, knowing if the leader needs the message at that moment or if it can wait. When you are not sure, indicate to your Leader that you have some information for him/her and wait for a response.

❖ Do not serve as a blockage to the people being ministered to by your leader. Your posture should be one of humility while keeping in mind that some folks will do anything to get an audience with your leader.

❖ Your posture should not change if you are rebuked by your leader. Try not to show body language or even give a response. There is a right time to address the matter or to use it as a lesson learnt.

- ❖ As you are serving, you may encounter your family and friends. Do not become distracted. Make sure that your leader is covered before socializing. There will be times when you are unable to connect with your family and friends. Simply let them know that you are working, and you will touch bases with them later.

- ❖ Keep your leader's information card handy; you may be asked for it. Also, have a notepad with a pen handy in the event you have to record information.

- ❖ Your Leader should not have to be told by someone else that something is out of place (his/her attire, for example). It is your job to check and double check that everything is in order!

- ❖ Do not allow your leader to go into the public unprepared. The leader is not only representing himself/herself but the body of Christ. Please speak up! Do this as humbly as you can.

- ❖ Do not allow your leader to drive alone if he/she is coming out of a high service. There will be times when you may need to accompany the leader home.

- ❖ Show up for your assignment. Give timely notice if you are unable to be in place so that other arrangements can be made. If there is more than one member of the team, communicate so that your leader is always covered.

- ❖ Be a good steward and pay your tithes and offerings.

- ❖ Choose to be an example in your action.

- ❖ Don't be slothful or slack concerning your oblations. Let your words be yes and amen.

❖ Do not become familiar with your leader. Give him/her the respect the position deserves.

Let the elder who rule well be counted worthy of double honor, especially those who labor in the word and doctrine.

1 Timothy 5:17

****

Reflection

1. What are some of the things you are doing now that you will have to change or enhance?

   ----

2. How has this chapter helped you?

   ----

3. Add items to your checklists.

Personal, Mental and Physical Preparation

Personal Evaluation

Make a self-evaluation. No one knows you better than you

do. You are called to be a servant/adjutant. This requires

you to work closely with the man/woman of God. Your life

should line up with your calling.

♦ Integrity is a standard that you display in everything you do.

There may be something in your life that you may have to

disregard, abandon, or even walk away from.

♦ Your life should exemplify to others around you that
you are living a life of holiness.

Mental Evaluation

In your serving, you should be sold out to your assignment. Others will see your elevation and realize that you are no longer hanging with them and will attempt to distract you. Stay focused; the call on your life has caused you to be elevated, so never mind the ill-spoken words.

❖ Continue to grow in God. As a songwriter penned: "Prove the doubters wrong; God is mighty and strong!"

❖ Know that prayer is your greatest weapon.

Or do you not know that your body is the temple of the Holy Spirit who is in you, whom you have from God, and you are not your own.

1 Corinthians 6:19

❖ Take your vitamins. You will need your physical strength to function at a high level.

❖ Stay healthy.

❖ Exercise your body and your mind.

❖ When you are not doing ministry, you do not have the right to adorn yourself unsightly or in a manner that does not represent the Kingdom.

****

Waiting on God's Timing

According to *Merriam-Webster* dictionary, timing is" **a choice, judgment, or control of when something should be done."**

It is:

1. A particular point or period of time when something should be done.

2. Placement or occurrence in time.

3. Observation and recording of the elapsed time of an act, action, or process.

The one phrase that stands out to me is the ability to choose the best moment for some action, movement. Every one of us, at some point in our lives, have questioned how to respond if we missed our timing.

Are we in the right place?

What should I be doing at this present time in my life?

Did I make the right decision in accepting the position?

Did I accept this assignment because I was given it or because I want the publicity?

Should I have said no, because I feel I am not qualified,

or my heart is leading me to work in another area?

Be guided by the scripture that says: "To everything there is a season and a time for every purpose under heaven" (Ecclesiastes 3:1). Verses 2 to 8 of this passage goes on to explain the different times and seasons; but, still, what does it all mean? We have to seek God and ask Him to direct us and show us the plans and purposes for our lives. He is the One with the master plan and the blueprint for our lives. He is the only one who can give us the right instruction for our destiny. Matthew 6:33 states: **"But seek ye first the Kingdom of GOD and His righteousness, and all these things shall be added unto you."**

Keys

❖ Speak to your spiritual leader/pastor for guidance and direction; he/she is the shepherd over your life and should be able to put things in perspective for you.

❖ Read up on and study any subject you are not unclear on.

❖ Speak with people who are presently working in that area. Don't be afraid to ask questions.

Waiting on GOD often feels long and drawn out but allow Him to direct your path. Sometimes we take matters into our own hands, and after we have messed up, we have to go right back to Him to help us. Not waiting leads to hardship and disappointment.

We find an example of this in Genesis 16. Sarai, Abram's wife, was unable to bear children, so she decided to give her maidservant Hagar to Abram to obtain children by her. God had already spoken to Abram and promised him a son, but he did not wait for God. Instead, he followed the reasoning of his wife and went into Hagar and she conceived. After she conceived, she looked down on her mistress, Sarai.

Sarai tried to help their situation and it turned out to be more of a disappointment and heartache. When we attempt to help God, it never works out in our favor. Allow God to do His perfect work and wait on His timing.

❖ In chapter 17, Sarai's name was changed to Sarah.

❖ In chapter 18, Sarah overheard that she was to have a son.

❖ In chapter 21, the LORD visited Sarah and she conceived.

This story gives us insight into what it means to wait on God.

The LORD is good unto them that wait for him, to the soul that seeketh Him.

Lamentations 3:25 KJV

As an armor-bearer, you have been chosen to work closely with your leader/man/woman of God. This is a call that you should hold in high regard. You must always serve with a spirit of excellence, using the opportunity as a training ground for the day you will be elevated as a leader and will want to be served with the same level of respect.

Keys

1. **Your prayer life will change**. The intercessor inside you has to be birthed for you to serve effectively. It is hard not to become an intercessor in this calling. The Father will reveal things to you that only you are anointed to accomplish and handle. As you seek Him and draw closer to Him, He will give you different strategies and give you the insight needed to function in your assignment. As a result, you will stand out from others.

2. **Prayer is Key**.

3. **Prayer changes the environment**.

4. **Prayer causes elevation**.

5. **Prayer gives you wisdom.**

6. **Fasting should be a part of your lifestyle**.

7. **Prayer gives you insights and direction.**

8. **Become acquainted with the different prayer watches or hours**.

These keys will help to bring and keep you in alignment with the will of God. Trust the man/woman of GOD that you are walking alongside. Just as you are praying for them, they are praying for you. Their spirit travels with you, and as you grow in ministry this will become more evident. People around you will begin to see the anointing of your leader being manifested in your life.

In the book of 2 Kings 5 is the story of how the servant of the man of God chose to walk in disobedience, but he did not realize that his spirit was with him. He

(Gehazi) allowed greed to control his thinking, and as a result, he and his descendants suffered for his bad decision.

Read the full chapter of 2 Kings 5.

<u>Keys</u>

❖ Remember that the choices you make will affect your life and those connected to you.

Make the right choices and good decisions.

❖ Make sure you invest in the man/woman of God. You should be the first person to bless your leader. This will yield dividends not only in your finances but in your health as well.

You have an awesome task ahead of you. Not only are you gifted, but in time you will also walk in the calling of a seer, to a degree. **Note: Not everyone can walk in the calling of a seer! This comes with time, prayer and fasting and a life surrendered and completely sold out unto God.**

You are your leader's eyes and ears. You are there to stop any device that is set in place to hinder the servant of God from annihilating the enemy's plans.

SHIFT!

The world we knew in 2019 has passed and brought changes, a new direction, and its own challenges. There will always be the need for the evangelist to echo the words "Jesus saves," and "the Kingdom of God is at hand." Each of us has the responsibility to build the Kingdom of God and to continue to be that light in the earth. You are called to be that armor-bearer. Stay on the assignment and the calling that you have been chosen to walk in, for you are God's armor-bearer. Currently, I am the armor-bearer to a vibrant, anointed vessel of God who serves alongside her husband as pastors of two churches in Freeport, Grand Bahama.

Prayer is at the forefront of her ministry. Pastor Shandlene Grant is an intercession who knows how to bombard the kingdom of darkness and speak the Word of

God with such power that it causes the gates of hell to release its hold on the one they attempted to hold captive.

I have walked closely with the Woman of God these past twenty-five-plus years. She walks in an apostolic anointing, something the body of Christ needs in this hour. This anointing has caused me to seek the face of God more intensely, to hear the voice of God and to be able to learn the difference between the prophetic and the apostolic gifts.

The style of these two pastors is dynamically different. Bishop is reserved while Lady G. is passionate in the way she wants things done correctly and expeditiously. Bishop's preaching style is bold and energetic, while Lady G. is a psalmist and a worshipper who will lead you into the presence of God and gently rest you at His feet with the sound of her voice.

Serving alongside this woman of God causes my prayer life to grow stronger. I have watched this bold warrior tell death to back off and I have seen people healed and delivered through her ministry. I have watched how she shifts the atmosphere and releases the sound of Heaven through her ministering in psalms.

As an armor-bearer you should also be walking in an anointing that matches that of the leader you are called to cover. You cannot be running away from a battle; you ought to be the one engaging in it. Be intentional about your serving.

Finally, my brethren, be strong in the Lord and in the power of His might. Put on the whole armor of GOD, that you may be able to stand against the wiles of the devil. For we do not wrestle against flesh and blood, but against principalities, against powers, against the rulers of the darkness of this age, against spiritual hosts of wickedness in the heavenly places. Therefore, take up

the whole armor of GOD, that you may be able to withstand in the evil day, and having done all, to stand. Stand therefore, having girded your waist with truth, having put on the breastplate of righteousness, and having shod your feet with the preparation of the gospel of peace; Above all, taking the shield of faith with which, you will be able to quench all the fiery darts of the wicked one. And take the helmet of salvation, and the sword of the Spirit, which is the word of God; Praying always with all prayer and supplication in the Spirit, being watchful to this end with all perseverance and supplication

for all the saints.

—Ephesians 6:10-18

As an armor-bearer you are considered a warrior. The above passage describes your weapons. We should be seen as armed and dangerous! When you enter a room people should sense you have come to do battle. Because you are walking with an anointing, you should be able to

76

engage and overcome anything that comes up against the assignment.

Worship should become a major part of your life. The Father is looking for those Kingdom dwellers to worship Him in spirit and in truth. The world we knew in 2019 has changed so drastically in 2020. What used to work for us then will not work now. The shift has taken place; therefore, our prayer life and worship have to intensify in this season. We can no longer depend on the preacher, the choir, or the church to connect us with the Master.

We need to have a personal relationship with God for ourselves. Learn how to win souls; read and study the scriptures so that when situations develop, His Word is on the inside of you and you can be a witness for Christ Jesus. Our Heavenly Father is calling for His manifested sons and daughters to take their rightful place in the earth. This is the hour that signs, wonders and miracles should be the order of the day. Let us stay connected to God and stay under the Open Heaven.

We are His representatives on the earth. We have to let our light shine—the light of Jesus—in this dark world. People are watching how we deal with situations; they need direction back to the Father. Yes, He has given you that awesome task to show and direct people back to the Savior. **You, yes you, are His greatness, armor-bearer, leading the lost to Christ.**

Reflection

How has this guide helped you as an armor-bearer or as one who is called to be an armor-bearer?

The Prayer

Father, it is in the name of Jesus we come to say "THANK YOU" for being our guide, Our Lord, and Master. We did not choose ourselves; You chose us before the foundation of the world. We ask for guidance. Proverbs 16:9 states that "a man's heart plans his ways; but the LORD directs   his steps." Lead us in the path of righteousness, cover us in Your love.

May we walk in Your will for our lives, in the name of Jesus. I ask You to watch over my leader now. Father give them the now Word for this assignment, that souls will come to know You as Lord and Master of their lives. Let Your power and glory fall now; heal, deliver and set free Your people. Proverb 16:25 says that "there is a way that seems right to a man, but its end is the way of death."

I decree and declare that the blood of Jesus covers the ears of the hearers, and their souls, minds and bodies will be saved. Your Word says to "seek ye first the kingdom of God, and His righteousness; and all these things shall be added unto you." I ask you, Father, to create in us a clean heart, O God, and renew a steadfast spirit within us. Restore unto us the joy of your salvation, for you are our God.

Bless us, keep us, and comfort us, for our help and strength cometh from You. Order our footsteps in Your Word, as we incline our ears to hear Your direction for our lives. Let Your Kingdom come and Your will be done. In the name of Jesus.

About the Author

Donnalee M. Peet, a woman of servitude and distinction. She has been a Servant in the field of Armor Bearers for the past twenty-five years. She has served in her home church,

(**C.O.G.O.P.**) as an Intercessor, and in the early nineties with the Hospitality Ministry praying for the sick before joining the Ministry Team of Evangelist Carnette Ferguson as an adjutant. After she transitioned to Mount Tabor Full Gospel Church, (Mount Tabor Church) in 1996 she joined the Fine Arts Ministry and also assisted with the Children's Ministry. She was a member of the choir and also on the Servants Board. She has been an Ambassador in the field of Tourism for the past thirty years providing Transportation Services to visitors around the island. This helped to prepare her for the transition to the Ministry of Helps at the church.

Under the supervision of her mentor Pastor Delton Ellis, she became the Director of Transportation at Mount Tabor Full Gospel Church. Her love for serving and seeing things done in excellence made this an easy task for her to accomplish. Mrs. Peet was also chosen to accompany one of the ministers of the Church on while assignments, where she then became her adjutant. She is still serving her up to this day.

This Servant of GOD is a Businesswoman, who holds an Associate of Arts in Christian Leadership. She is married to her faithful partner of 15 years, Mr. Wesley L. Peet Sr., and has two sons Danny Jr. And Dinero. She also has four grandsons. She and her husband reside on the beautiful Island of Grand Bahama in the Bahamas.

Contact Information

Donnalee M. Peet

P. O. Box F-41324

Freeport, Grand Bahama

The Bahamas

Phone Contact: 1 242 431-5604

Email Address: donnaleepeet@gmail.com

Facebook: facebook.com/donnalee.peet